T0207660

Zooey goes to Heaven.

Helping a Child Cope with the Death of a Pet

By Joseph Venturelli

For Barbara, Michael, ToniAnn and Uncle Sonny

Order this book online at www.trafford.com
or email orders@trafford.com

Most Trafford titles are also available at major online book retailers.

 www.trafford.com

North America & international
toll-free: 844 688 6899 (USA & Canada)
fax: 812 355 4082

Our mission is to efficiently provide the world's finest, most comprehensive book publishing service, enabling every author to experience success. To find out how to publish your book, your way, and have it available worldwide, visit us online at www.trafford.com

Because of the dynamic nature of the Internet, any web addresses or links contained in this book may have changed since publication and may no longer be valid. The views expressed in this work are solely those of the author and do not necessarily reflect the views of the publisher, and the publisher hereby disclaims any responsibility for them.

Any people depicted in stock imagery provided by Getty Images are models, and such images are being used for illustrative purposes only.
Certain stock imagery © Getty Images.

ISBN: 978-1-4120-7683-8 (sc)

Print information available on the last page.

Trafford rev. 08/03/2021

My Name is ToniAnn,

I have two dogs, I call them Rummels and Zooey.

Rummels and Zooey

have been in my house

since before I was born.

They are **best friends** and play together all the time.

Rummels
is much bigger than Zooey,

but **Zooey** is much older.

Zooey is getting **very old...**

Mommy has been taking **Zooey**
to the **doggy doctor** a lot.

Daddy says Zooey is not feeling very well.

Rummels licks Zooeys face when he is **feeling bad**

My Uncle was not feeling very well last year and he went to heaven and Mommy says he is feeling better now that he is in heaven.

Mommy and Daddy say
that Zooey will be **in Heaven soon** with my Uncle.

Today

I came home from school and Mommy and Daddy said

that Zooey was feeling too sick and **he went to heaven** to feel better.

Me and Rummels **really miss** Zooey, but I am happy he is feeling better.

Printed in the United States
by Baker & Taylor Publisher Services